I0196027

N.I.C.H.E.

Now I can Have EVERYTHING

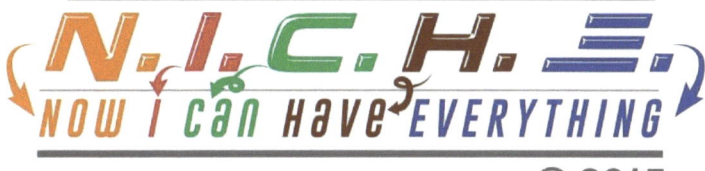

INTRODUCTION

Allow me to clarify what 'Everything' represents:

"Everything is anything that has true worth / value to you."

"The bottom line is *not* money; **the bottom line is A QUALITY LIFE!**"

– Dr. Charlene Nelson

Our end goal is not to acquire things, or notoriety, or produce a long resume of accomplishments. The target of the N.I.C.H.E. concept is to live out a QUALITY LIFE successfully, consistently.

OBSERVATION

I've come to realize people spend countless days of the year living in a heavy fog without pursuing their life's passion or pursuing aspirations for their betterment, only to build up some type of false momentum around the New Year. Resolutions are then declared that disappointments felt throughout the current year will not be the case in the next year. Question: How is that even remotely possible when there is not a plan in place to destroy the stagnation of any unproductive lifestyle patterns? Many New Year's Resolutions are abandoned within the first 10 days and before you realize it you're at the mid-year point and then, somewhere around December you'll hear yourself saying things like, "This year has flown by!" For many of us, major disappointment begins to make its unwelcomed appearance yet again. We have to be intentional in not allowing this type of fruitlessness to continue; it wears on you internally because it's ultimately a dead end. You can't afford to ignore the deep gnawing inside of you. Regardless of how many times we've heard it, life is lived one day (or more specifically) one moment at a time. Stewardship of your time is as crucial to your success as being a good steward of your finances. Time is a commodity, trade it well.

REALIZATION

I read a poignant statement, "<u>People want progress but hate change</u>."

Recently, there has been nonstop construction on some waterfront properties near my home because the properties are terribly underdeveloped. There is now no shortage of cranes, massive building equipment, trucks, planners, workers and last but certainly not least, noise; extreme ongoing noise. As a publisher / author I do a good portion of my work from my home office so when this major project began, I was concerned about not being able to control the amount of disturbance outside. Then one day as I was looking out and watching the volume of activity it dawned on me that this temporary inconvenience is going to produce several positive benefits: 1) increase the value of our property, 2) increase the value of the neighborhood, 3) bring needed resources to our district, 4) ultimately enhance the quality of the environment and the privileges my husband and I desired when choosing this location we call home. Do I like the constant noise? NO. Do I like the ongoing diversions of traffic; for vehicles and pedestrians? NO. Do I like seeing all the eyesores the construction warrants? NO. Yet, all of this is temporary and more importantly, necessary. On that day of contemplation, my MIND changed when I understood we were experiencing – <u>TRUE PROGRESS</u>. Not just noise, inconvenience or disturbance; but TRUE PROGRESS. Now, that epiphany has yielded a tolerance and dare I say an appreciation for the activities that were once a serious source of irritation. Jim Rohn insightfully said, "*Your life does not get better by chance. It gets better by change.*"

ADAPTATION

If you want to see your life progressively move forward there has to be change; there is no way around it. Remember, you will always get what you have if you always do what you've done. Our perspectives need to be examined if we cannot handle the transition of change well, whether it's your decision or something beyond your control. One of the clear ways to determine if change is required, ask yourself: Does this change mean the quality of my life will be improved or the goal(s) I have in mind accomplished?

The 'Everything' in 'N.I.C.H.E. – Now I Can Have Everything' has to be kept in context for this concept to really work. ***'Everything' is not acquisition or consumption but rather the development of a creative and unlimited stream of purposeful living; an ongoing endeavor.*** Question: How bad do you want it? This means you have to get fed up with accepting disappointment and reducing it by saying, "It is what it is."

Think about what's at stake, you know you could have made definitive progress had a plan been in place. Does it mean you may have to shake up your otherwise predictable life to initiate the change you so desperately need? YES! If it's EVER going to happen, it starts with YOU! Change is inevitable, so wouldn't it be great if it was incorporated in your life's blueprint as opposed to being something you're forced to accept. Progress cannot come without change. Components of 'True Progress' are accurate estimation, development, growth, focus, innovation, strength gained, steps forward, detailed insight, fruition, increase and fulfillment.

CONCENTRATION

For some, you're good with change. You actually welcome it but the results never quite equal your goals and expectations. You're flexible, you're committed but you lack FOCUS. Focus renders the clarity, understanding, discipline and courage necessary to orchestrate an *effective* change. Bad or lazy habits, pressure and fear of the unknown are enemies of change; not always consciously but they are nonetheless.

No matter what, **stay FOCUSED**. You want to see otherwise calm folk get riled up?...announce a change in their routine; instant rebellion followed by a tornado of resistance swells into a tsunami of resentment. Sounds overstated, it's not. Businesses, organizations and yes, even families have come apart because change was needed but never embraced. Question: Have you ever died slowly inside because you knew the changes needed were being ignored to 'keep the peace?' Only to see an eerily slow version of decay because change was rejected. But at what cost? Often, it cost us dearly including the joy of living and loving?

IMPLEMENTATION

We've got to remove the options of resistance, mediocrity, fear, insolence and paralysis as it pertains to the lives we desire to live. Many of us, if we're honest have at some time been 'walking dead.' Dead in principle, dead in hope, dead in creativity, dead in effort. We allow ourselves to become fixtures when we should be inventive problem solvers prepared to assist in fixing many of life's ills. We complain but that's almost illegal if you're unwilling to do something about it. We should all be disgusted with hearing the lame excuse, "I'm just one person." Lame excuse! One person can inspire change simply by refusing to operate under the old systematic way especially if that way is doing more harm than good. Are we suggesting a riot? Or disregard for those in your surroundings? Absolutely not! However, we are encouraging you to get a real understanding of your life's passion and goal…right now. Why waste another minute conforming when you can be an agent of change and initiate true progress? It starts with your mind; do not deny the arrival of the very answers you seek. They are right in front of you but you can suffocate them with excuses, justifications, inactivity or silence.

ACTUALIZATION

Everything that matters to you is hanging in the balance until you gather yourself and determine to identify your place in this world. Insist on finding your niche, once you do your life will confidently speak – **"_Now_ I Can Have Everything!"**

EVALUATION

As you journey to your N.I.C.H.E. remember the vital components of 'True Progress':

COMPONENTS	REFERENCE OF LESSONS LEARNED
1. Accurate Estimation	
2. Development	
3. Growth	
4. Focus	
5. Innovation	
6. Strength Gained	
7. Solid Steps Forward	
8. Detailed Insight	
9. Fruition	
10. Increase	
11. Fulfilment	

Whenever we're presented with new opportunities or scenarios, we often think about our liabilities and weaknesses rather than focus on our assets. We want to train you to a greater degree of confidence in who you are and what you can offer to *any* situation.

We're not simply here to make you feel good; we're here to partner with you in seeing the viable possibilities in getting the life you want.

© Dr. Charlene Nelson ~ Build Forward

© 2015

Get your 'N.I.C.H.E.' underway or refine it now!

202.714.7724

*"The two most important days in your life are the **day** you are **born** and the **day** you find out **why**."*

– Mark Twain

ABOUT THE AUTHOR

Dr. Charlene Nelson is an author, publisher, speaker, master coach & business owner. Charlene's business dynamic is fortified with a wealth of experience and knowledge; successfully practiced for over 28 years. "GET THE LIFE YOU WANT" Dr. Nelson's innovative program assists audiences worldwide in tackling real life challenges with 'doable' strategies. For focused participants: purpose identified + accomplished goals = proven results.

'The N.I.C.H.E. Concept' provides a clear process complemented by practical tools for everyone who wants answers for successful living.

Dr. Nelson exuberantly shares love, life and business with her husband, Dale.

EVALUATION

As you journey to your **N.I.C.H.E.** remember the vital components of 'True Progress':

COMPONENTS	REFERENCE OF LESSONS LEARNED

1. Accurate Estimation

2. Development

3. Growth

4. Focus

5. Innovation

6. Strength Gained

7. Solid Steps Forward

8. Detailed Insight

9. Fruition

10. Increase

11. Fulfilment

EVALUATION

As you journey to your **N.I.C.H.E.** remember the vital components of 'True Progress':

| COMPONENTS | REFERENCE OF LESSONS LEARNED |

1. Accurate Estimation

2. Development

3. Growth

4. Focus

5. Innovation

6. Strength Gained

7. Solid Steps Forward

8. Detailed Insight

9. Fruition

10. Increase

11. Fulfilment

© 2015

EVALUATION

As you journey to your **N.I.C.H.E.** remember the vital components of 'True Progress':

| COMPONENTS | REFERENCE OF LESSONS LEARNED |

1. Accurate Estimation

2. Development

3. Growth

4. Focus

5. Innovation

6. Strength Gained

7. Solid Steps Forward

8. Detailed Insight

9. Fruition

10. Increase

11. Fulfilment

EVALUATION

As you journey to your **N.I.C.H.E.** remember the vital components of 'True Progress':

COMPONENTS	REFERENCE OF LESSONS LEARNED

1. **Accurate Estimation**

2. **Development**

3. **Growth**

4. **Focus**

5. **Innovation**

6. **Strength Gained**

7. **Solid Steps Forward**

8. **Detailed Insight**

9. **Fruition**

10. **Increase**

11. **Fulfilment**

© 2015

EVALUATION

As you journey to your **N.I.C.H.E.** remember the vital components of 'True Progress':

COMPONENTS	REFERENCE OF LESSONS LEARNED

1. Accurate Estimation

2. Development

3. Growth

4. Focus

5. Innovation

6. Strength Gained

7. Solid Steps Forward

8. Detailed Insight

9. Fruition

10. Increase

11. Fulfilment

EVALUATION

As you journey to your **N.I.C.H.E.** remember the vital components of 'True Progress':

COMPONENTS	REFERENCE OF LESSONS LEARNED

1. Accurate Estimation

2. Development

3. Growth

4. Focus

5. Innovation

6. Strength Gained

7. Solid Steps Forward

8. Detailed Insight

9. Fruition

10. Increase

11. Fulfilment

EVALUATION

As you journey to your **N.I.C.H.E.** remember the vital components of 'True Progress':

COMPONENTS	REFERENCE OF LESSONS LEARNED

1. Accurate Estimation

2. Development

3. Growth

4. Focus

5. Innovation

6. Strength Gained

7. Solid Steps Forward

8. Detailed Insight

9. Fruition

10. Increase

11. Fulfilment

EVALUATION

As you journey to your **N.I.C.H.E.** remember the vital components of 'True Progress':

COMPONENTS	REFERENCE OF LESSONS LEARNED

1. Accurate Estimation

2. Development

3. Growth

4. Focus

5. Innovation

6. Strength Gained

7. Solid Steps Forward

8. Detailed Insight

9. Fruition

10. Increase

11. Fulfilment

EVALUATION

As you journey to your **N.I.C.H.E.** remember the vital components of 'True Progress':

COMPONENTS	REFERENCE OF LESSONS LEARNED

1. Accurate Estimation

2. Development

3. Growth

4. Focus

5. Innovation

6. Strength Gained

7. Solid Steps Forward

8. Detailed Insight

9. Fruition

10. Increase

11. Fulfilment

© 2015

EVALUATION

As you journey to your **N.I.C.H.E.** remember the vital components of 'True Progress':

COMPONENTS	REFERENCE OF LESSONS LEARNED

1. **Accurate Estimation**

2. **Development**

3. **Growth**

4. **Focus**

5. **Innovation**

6. **Strength Gained**

7. **Solid Steps Forward**

8. **Detailed Insight**

9. **Fruition**

10. **Increase**

11. **Fulfilment**

EVALUATION

As you journey to your **N.I.C.H.E.** remember the vital components of 'True Progress':

COMPONENTS   REFERENCE OF LESSONS LEARNED

1. Accurate Estimation
2. Development
3. Growth
4. Focus
5. Innovation
6. Strength Gained
7. Solid Steps Forward
8. Detailed Insight
9. Fruition
10. Increase
11. Fulfilment

EVALUATION

As you journey to your **N.I.C.H.E.** remember the vital components of 'True Progress':

COMPONENTS	REFERENCE OF LESSONS LEARNED
1. Accurate Estimation	
2. Development	
3. Growth	
4. Focus	
5. Innovation	
6. Strength Gained	
7. Solid Steps Forward	
8. Detailed Insight	
9. Fruition	
10. Increase	
11. Fulfilment	

EVALUATION

As you journey to your **N.I.C.H.E.** remember the vital components of 'True Progress':

COMPONENTS	REFERENCE OF LESSONS LEARNED

1. Accurate Estimation

2. Development

3. Growth

4. Focus

5. Innovation

6. Strength Gained

7. Solid Steps Forward

8. Detailed Insight

9. Fruition

10. Increase

11. Fulfilment

EVALUATION

As you journey to your **N.I.C.H.E.** remember the vital components of 'True Progress':

COMPONENTS	REFERENCE OF LESSONS LEARNED

1. Accurate Estimation

2. Development

3. Growth

4. Focus

5. Innovation

6. Strength Gained

7. Solid Steps Forward

8. Detailed Insight

9. Fruition

10. Increase

11. Fulfilment

EVALUATION

As you journey to your **N.I.C.H.E.** remember the vital components of 'True Progress':

COMPONENTS	REFERENCE OF LESSONS LEARNED

1. Accurate Estimation

2. Development

3. Growth

4. Focus

5. Innovation

6. Strength Gained

7. Solid Steps Forward

8. Detailed Insight

9. Fruition

10. Increase

11. Fulfilment

EVALUATION

As you journey to your **N.I.C.H.E.** remember the vital components of 'True Progress':

COMPONENTS	REFERENCE OF LESSONS LEARNED

1. Accurate Estimation

2. Development

3. Growth

4. Focus

5. Innovation

6. Strength Gained

7. Solid Steps Forward

8. Detailed Insight

9. Fruition

10. Increase

11. Fulfilment

EVALUATION

As you journey to your **N.I.C.H.E.** remember the vital components of 'True Progress':

COMPONENTS	REFERENCE OF LESSONS LEARNED

1. **Accurate Estimation**

2. **Development**

3. **Growth**

4. **Focus**

5. **Innovation**

6. **Strength Gained**

7. **Solid Steps Forward**

8. **Detailed Insight**

9. **Fruition**

10. **Increase**

11. **Fulfilment**

EVALUATION

As you journey to your **N.I.C.H.E.** remember the vital components of 'True Progress':

COMPONENTS	REFERENCE OF LESSONS LEARNED

1. **Accurate Estimation**

2. **Development**

3. **Growth**

4. **Focus**

5. **Innovation**

6. **Strength Gained**

7. **Solid Steps Forward**

8. **Detailed Insight**

9. **Fruition**

10. **Increase**

11. **Fulfilment**

© 2015

EVALUATION

As you journey to your **N.I.C.H.E.** remember the vital components of 'True Progress':

COMPONENTS	REFERENCE OF LESSONS LEARNED
1. Accurate Estimation	
2. Development	
3. Growth	
4. Focus	
5. Innovation	
6. Strength Gained	
7. Solid Steps Forward	
8. Detailed Insight	
9. Fruition	
10. Increase	
11. Fulfilment	

EVALUATION

As you journey to your N.I.C.H.E. remember the vital components of 'True Progress':

| COMPONENTS | REFERENCE OF LESSONS LEARNED |

1. Accurate Estimation

2. Development

3. Growth

4. Focus

5. Innovation

6. Strength Gained

7. Solid Steps Forward

8. Detailed Insight

9. Fruition

10. Increase

11. Fulfilment

EVALUATION

As you journey to your **N.I.C.H.E.** remember the vital components of 'True Progress':

COMPONENTS	REFERENCE OF LESSONS LEARNED

1. Accurate Estimation

2. Development

3. Growth

4. Focus

5. Innovation

6. Strength Gained

7. Solid Steps Forward

8. Detailed Insight

9. Fruition

10. Increase

11. Fulfilment

EVALUATION

As you journey to your **N.I.C.H.E.** remember the vital components of 'True Progress':

COMPONENTS	REFERENCE OF LESSONS LEARNED

1. Accurate Estimation

2. Development

3. Growth

4. Focus

5. Innovation

6. Strength Gained

7. Solid Steps Forward

8. Detailed Insight

9. Fruition

10. Increase

11. Fulfilment

EVALUATION

As you journey to your **N.I.C.H.E.** remember the vital components of 'True Progress':

COMPONENTS	REFERENCE OF LESSONS LEARNED

1. **Accurate Estimation**

2. **Development**

3. **Growth**

4. **Focus**

5. **Innovation**

6. **Strength Gained**

7. **Solid Steps Forward**

8. **Detailed Insight**

9. **Fruition**

10. **Increase**

11. **Fulfilment**

EVALUATION

As you journey to your **N.I.C.H.E.** remember the vital components of 'True Progress':

COMPONENTS	REFERENCE OF LESSONS LEARNED

1. Accurate Estimation

2. Development

3. Growth

4. Focus

5. Innovation

6. Strength Gained

7. Solid Steps Forward

8. Detailed Insight

9. Fruition

10. Increase

11. Fulfilment

EVALUATION

As you journey to your **N.I.C.H.E.** remember the vital components of 'True Progress':

COMPONENTS	REFERENCE OF LESSONS LEARNED

1. Accurate Estimation

2. Development

3. Growth

4. Focus

5. Innovation

6. Strength Gained

7. Solid Steps Forward

8. Detailed Insight

9. Fruition

10. Increase

11. Fulfilment

© 2015

EVALUATION

As you journey to your **N.I.C.H.E.** remember the vital components of 'True Progress':

COMPONENTS   REFERENCE OF LESSONS LEARNED

1. Accurate Estimation

2. Development

3. Growth

4. Focus

5. Innovation

6. Strength Gained

7. Solid Steps Forward

8. Detailed Insight

9. Fruition

10. Increase

11. Fulfilment

© 2015

www.ingramcontent.com/pod-product-compliance
Lightning Source LLC
Chambersburg PA
CBHW041813040426
42450CB00001B/22